AMOUR

# AMOUR

## a photographic celebration

MQP
MQ Publications Ltd

Give all to love, obey thy heart.

*Ralph Waldo Emerson*

In short I will part with anything for you, but you.

*Lady Mary Wortley Montagu*

There is only one kind of love,

but there are a thousand

different versions.

*François, Duc de La Rochefoucauld*

Oh that it were possible

After long grief and pain

To find the arms of my true love,

Round me once again!

*Alfred, Lord Tennyson*

Love conquers all things:

let us too surrender to love.

*Virgil*

We love being in love,

that's the truth of it.

*William Makepeace Thackeray*

A heart that loves is always young.

*Greek proverb*

I like not only to be loved,

but to be told I am loved.

*George Eliot*

A lover without indiscretion

is no lover at all.

*Thomas Hardy*

At the touch of love everyone becomes a poet.

*Plato*

There is only one happiness in life,

to love and be loved.

*George Sand*

Love, as told by the seers of old,

Comes as a butterfly tipped with gold.

Flutters and flies in sunlight skies,

Weaving round hearts that were one time cold.

*Algernon Charles Swinburne*

Words are only painted fire; a look is the fire itself.

*Mark Twain*

There is no difficulty that love will not conquer...

*Emmet Fox*

All love is sweet,

Given or returned.

*Percy Bysshe Shelley*

Love one another and you will be happy.

It's as simple and as difficult as that.

*Michael Leunig*

Age does not protect

you from love but love

to some extent protects

you from age.

*Jeanne Moreau*

Do you want me to tell you something really subversive? Love is everything it's cracked up to be. That's why people are so cynical about it. It really is worth fighting for, being brave for, risking everything for. And the trouble is if you don't risk anything, you risk even more.

*Erica Jong*

Soul meets soul on lovers' lips.

*Percy Bysshe Shelley*

Speech happens not to be his language.

*Madame de Staël*

In the Spring

a livelier iris changes

on the burnish'd dove;

In the Spring

a young man's fancy

turns to thoughts of love.

*Alfred, Lord Tennyson*

We are all born for love.

It is the principle of existence,

and its only end.

*Benjamin Disraeli*

True, we love life, not because

we are used to living, but

because we are used to loving.

There is always some madness

in love, but there is also always

some reason in madness.

*Fredrich Nietzsche*

We should count time by heart-throbs.

*P. J. Bailey*

I have seen only you,

I have admired only you,

I desire only you.

*Napoleon Bonaparte*

I hate all that don't love me, and slight all that do.

*George Farquhar*

Love is love's reward.

*John Dryden*

Love vanquishes time.

To lovers, a moment

can be eternity,

eternity can be the

tick of a clock.

*Mary Parrish*

Gravitation cannot be held

responsible for people

falling in love.

*Albert Einstein*

What happiness to be beloved; and O,

What bliss, ye gods, to love!

*Johann Wolfgang Goethe*

Who so loves

Believes the impossible.

*Elizabeth Barrett Browning*

Love consists in this,

that two solitudes

protect and border

and salute each other.

*Rainer Maria Rilke*

If any person wish to be idle,

let them fall in love.

*Jack Mulhall*

The magic of first love

is our ignorance that

it can never end.

*Benjamin Disraeli*

True love comes quietly, without banners or flashing lights. If you hear bells, get your ears checked.

*Edith Segal*

Love means the body, the soul, the life, the entire being. We feel love as we feel the warmth of our blood, we breathe love as we breathe air, we hold it in ourselves as we hold our thoughts. Nothing more exists for us.

*Guy de Maupassant*

The world has little to bestow

Where two fond hearts in equal love are joined.

*Anna Laetitia Barbauld*

Love doesn't make the world
go 'round. Love is what
makes the ride worthwhile.

*Franklin P. Jones*

Love is made by two people,

in different kinds of solitude.

It can be in a crowd,

but in an oblivious crowd.

*Louis Aragon*

Love does not consist

in gazing at each other,

but in looking outward

in the same direction.

*Antoine de Saint-Exupéry*

Passion is the element in which we live;

without it, we hardly vegetate.

*Lord Byron*

Being deeply loved by someone gives you strength,

while loving someone deeply gives you courage.

*Lao-Tzu*

If there is anything better

than to be loved,

it is loving.

*Anonymous*

True love is like a ghost:

everybody talks about it

but few have seen it.

*François, Duc de La Rochefoucauld*

To live is like to love—

all reason is against it,

and all healthy instinct is for it.

*Samuel Butler*

It is wrong to think that love comes from long companionship and preserving courtship. Love is the offspring of spiritual affinity and unless that affinity is created in a moment, it will not be created for years or even generations.

*Kahlil Gibran*

Love is but the discovery of

ourselves in others, and the

delight in the recognition.

*Alexander Smith*

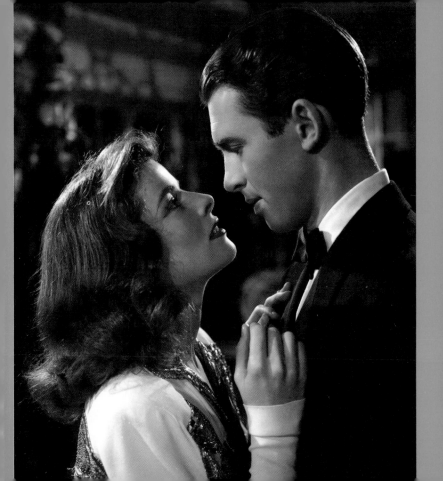

Oh,

what a dear

ravishing thing

is the beginning

of an amour!

*Aphra Behn*

Harmony is pure love,

for love is complete agreement.

*Lope de Vega*

Love is the only game that is not

called on account of darkness.

*Anonymous*

Try to reason with love and

you will lose your reason.

*French proverb*

If I had never met him I would have

dreamed him into being.

*Anzia Yezierska*

I have enjoyed

the happiness of the world;

I have lived and loved.

*Johann Friedrich von Schiller*

# Picture Credits

cover: Cabaret dancers Wes Adams and Lisa, 1937.

title page: A sailor bids a passionate farewell to his sweetheart, 1945.

page 4: Actress Mary Ure and Paul Scofield in a scene from the play "Time Remembered," 1955.

page 6: A sailor bids a passionate farewell to his sweetheart, 1945.

page 9: A courting couple sit arm in arm in Hyde Park, London, 1947.

page 10: A woman greeting her Skymaster Aircrew husband with enthusiasm, 1958.

page 13: Barbara Stanwyck and David Niven in the film "The Other Love" directed by Andre de Toth, 1947.

page 14: A couple kissing while sitting on the banks of the Seine, 1952.

page 16: Sydney nightclub dancer Marlene Hall relaxes at Bondi beach, 1956.

page 18: Billie Dove and Australian actor, George Andre Bernager in "The Age For Love" directed by Frank Lloyd, 1931.

page 21: Two pairs of feet, one male, one female, meet underneath the table, 1928.

page 23: Honeymooners hold hands as they enjoy a drink in their honeymoon hotel, 1956.

page 24: A young couple watch the waves rolling in, 1955.

page 26: John Gilbert has an affair with local French girl

Renée Adorée in the drama "The Big Parade," 1925.

page 29: A bartender waits attentively on a young couple out on a date, 1955.

page 30: A well-balanced couple enjoying a kiss while water-skiing,1962.

page 32: American leading man Richard Arlen seen with his wife Jobyna Halston relaxing in a tree in their Toluca Lake home, circa 1935.

page 35: A bride and groom kiss in the back seat of a car, circa 1955 © LR Legwin/Hulton Archive

page 36: Mr and Mrs Leake celebrate their diamond wedding, 1929.

page 38: A soldier of the British Expeditionary Force is greeted by his girlfriend, 1940.

page 41: Headshot of a man and woman kissing while she reclines, circa 1945 © Camerique/Hulton Archive.

page 42: American film stars Fay Wray and Gary Cooper in a passionate embrace, 1928.

page 44: A couple lying arm in arm on the banks of the River Seine in Paris, 1952.

page 47: A young man serenades his sweetheart with a guitar on a rocky promontory of Tonga, an island in the Pacific Ocean, 1953 © Ernst Haas/Hulton Archive.

page 47: Cast members relax between dance rehearsals for the film "West Side Story," 1960.

page 51: Actors Nicholas Nannen and Mary Glynne from the play "Accent On Youth," 1935.

page 52: US actor Rod LaRocque and Rita La Roy in a scene from the film "The Delightful Rogue," circa 1925.

page 55: Mandy Rice-Davies at the press launch of her book "The Mandy Report," 1963.

page 57: Shop girl Lucy Pereira spends a romantic day on Ipanema Beach in Rio de Janeiro, 1950.

page 58: A young couple in front of the Houses of Parliament, London, 1967.

page 61: World trampolining champion Paul Luxon and his fiancée, German Ladies Champion Ute Czech, 1973.

page 62: Janet Jones, a secretary undergoing training for a career in modelling, embraces a fellow model, 1954.

page 65: Tyrone Power and Rita Hayworth in "Blood and Sand," 1941.

page 66: A young courting couple returning from a social engagement, 1953.

page 68: American actor Jack Mulhall in a beach scene with actress Dorothy Mackaill, circa 1932.

page 70: A boy sits and carves a heart beneath his initials on a tree trunk, using a small knife, circa 1945.

page 72: A couple relaxing in a basement in Elephant and Castle, South London, 1949.

page 75: Two lovers caught in a tight embrace on New York's Coney Island Beach at night-time, circa 1943 © Weegee/International Centre of Photography.

page 76: A couple sit on the Thames embankment with Tower Bridge in the background, 1954.

page 79: A young couple at Waterloo Station, 1955.

page 81: Eleanor Powell and James Stewart in a scene from the musical "Born To Dance," 1936.

page 82: A courting couple embrace, overlooking the promenade and beach on the Isle of Man, 1939.

page 85: A couple kiss in the Louvre, Paris, 1947.

page 86: A couple on their honeymoon look out over a lake in Switzerland, 1948.

page 88: Couple kissing under mistletoe during a Christmas party for the Flying Fortress Boys, 1942.

page 91: A couple pressing their hands against a pane of glass which is separating them, 1954.

page 93: Two lonely hearts meet in the park of the Villa Borghese in Rome, 1956.

page 94: A young couple in an anti-Le Pen demonstration in Paris, 1993 © Steve Eason/Hulton Archive.

page 97: Katharine Hepburn and James Stewart in "The Philadelphia Story," directed by George Cukor, 1940.

page 99: Clark Gable and Constance Bennet star in "After Office Hours," 1934.

page 100: A tourist couple sitting by Niagara Falls, 1961.

page 102: Teenager Betty Burden and her date standing together on a dimly-lit street in Birmingham, 1951.

page 105: A couple kissing on Bastille Day on the steps of Montmartre, Paris, 1950.

page 106: British actress Olivia Hussey and actor Leonard Whiting star in Franco Zeffrelli's Romeo and Juliet, 1967.

page 108: Bert and Ellie Lang, a young couple on their honeymoon in Hawaii, circa 1955.

Published by MQ Publications Limited
12 The Ivories, 6–8 Northampton Street, London, N1 2HY
Tel: 020 7359 2244 / Fax: 020 7359 1616
e-mail: mail@mqpublications.com

ISBN: 1-84072-174-X

1 3 5 7 9 0 8 6 4 2

Cover design: John Casey
Design: Philippa Jarvis
Series Editor: Elizabeth Carr

Printed and bound in China